M000304718

WHERE IS THE
PROMISE OF
HIS COMING?

DESTINY IMAGE BOOKS BY JOHN AND CAROL ARNOTT

The Spirit and Bride Say, "Come!"

Preparing for the Glory

Essential Training for Preparing for the Glory

Soaking in the Spirit

Grace and Forgiveness

Soaking Encounter Journal

WHERE IS THE
PROMISE OF
HIS COMING?

PROPHETIC SIGNPOSTS POINTING TO
THE SOON RETURN OF JESUS

JOHN ARNOTT

© Copyright 2022—John Arnott

All rights reserved. This book is protected by the copyright laws of the United States of America. This book may not be copied or reprinted for commercial gain or profit. The use of short quotations or occasional page copying for personal or group study is permitted and encouraged. Permission will be granted upon request. Unless otherwise identified, Scripture quotations are taken from the New King James Version. Copyright © 1982 by Thomas Nelson, Inc. Used by permission. All rights reserved. Scripture quotations marked ESV are taken from The Holy Bible, English Standard Version® (ESV®), copyright © 2001 by Crossway, a publishing ministry of Good News Publishers. Used by permission. All rights reserved. Scripture quotations marked KJV are taken from the King James Version. All emphasis within Scripture quotations is the author's own. Please note that Destiny Image's publishing style capitalizes certain pronouns that refer to the Father, Son, and Holy Spirit, and may differ from some publishers' styles. Take note that the name satan and related names are not capitalized. We choose not to acknowledge him, even to the point of violating grammatical rules.

DESTINY IMAGE® PUBLISHERS, INC.
P.O. Box 310, Shippensburg, PA 17257-0310
"Promoting Inspired Lives."

This book and all other Destiny Image and Destiny Image Fiction books are available at Christian bookstores and distributors worldwide.

For more information on foreign distributors, call 717-532-3040.
Reach us on the Internet: www.destinyimage.com.

ISBN 13 TP: 978-0-7684-6459-7
ISBN 13 eBook: 978-0-7684-6460-3

For Worldwide Distribution, Printed in the U.S.A.
1 2 3 4 5 6 7 8 / 26 25 24 23 22

CONTENTS

FOREWORD

In *Where Is the Promise of His Coming?* John Arnott links the headlines of today with the prophecies of the Bible. John's book is a master class in end-time prophecy. As Christians, we need to be aware of all the prophecies being fulfilled in our day so that we can encourage each other with the promises of God.

Jesus wants to return and return soon. There are two conditions on His return. The first is found in Matthew 24:14: "*And this gospel of the kingdom will be preached in all the world as a witness to all the nations, and then the end will come.*" The Church is getting very close to completing the Great Commission, and we should redouble our efforts to reach every nation, tribe, and tongue in our generation. Let us all imitate the lives of John and Carol Arnott and go to every continent to bring witness to the power of God.

The second condition to Christ's return should give us all pause; the number of martyrs has not yet been completed. In Revelation 6:9-11, the apostle John wrote:

> *I saw under the altar the souls of those who had been slain for the word of God and for the testimony which they held. And they cried with a loud voice, saying, "How long, O Lord, holy and true, until You judge and avenge our blood on those who dwell on the earth?" Then a white robe was given to each of them; and it was said to them that they should rest a little while longer, until both the number of their fellow servants and their brethren, who would be killed as they were, was completed.*

As we draw nearer to the return of the Messiah, realize that God wants to reveal His miraculous power and glory through ordinary people like you and me—people who have faith in Him. We are waiting for Him, and He is waiting for us. He is waiting for us to take the risk of faith and put our trust in Him even when everything seems hopeless. The problems of our day were predicted long ago just so that we would have the faith to believe. These things are happening so the glory of the Lord would be revealed and God's name would be magnified among all people. Let us look to the heavens, for our redemption is drawing nigh.

—Gordon Robertson
President, the Christian Broadcasting Network

INTRODUCTION

I really believe that the message of the soon return of Christ is a subject that the Christian community needs to move to center stage at this crucial time in history. The world has been filled with wars, famines, and various problems for many hundreds of years, and yet in today's world, disasters seem to be multiplying exponentially. I believe it is vital that the Church be the purveyors of good news, even the best news, for a world that is drowning in fake news, spin, and disaster stories, all with zero hope for the suffering and for the ones observing and caring.

The return of Jesus for those who long for righteousness, peace, and truth is actually the best news ever, fulfilling promises, hopes, and dreams that have been deep longings in human hearts for millennia. So get ready, friends, it won't be long until all these promises are concluded!

This short eschatology is not meant to be comprehensive, across the board, or adequately discussing all aspects of this vast topic. We are merely trying to wake people up to the many current signs and ancient prophecies now fulfilled and recently fulfilled, which clearly tell us that we are in the final days before the imminent return to the earth of the Lord Jesus Christ. His return, rule, and reign is the ultimate completion of man's six thousand years of recorded history on earth.

Please read this book with an open, teachable mind. Be willing to put your previous understandings and theologies to one side for a moment so as to have fresh consideration of this all-important subject. The implications of biblical eschatology are far too important to allow us to remain indifferent or to hold personal strong opinions that prefer one particular point of view. We need to be willing to try to learn from each other, constantly reviewing our position so that we are more likely to get things right and be better prepared for what is soon to take place.

God bless you as you strengthen your heart for the greatest event since the Creation of the world—the return of King Jesus to rule and reign on planet earth.

—John Arnott

1

GOD'S ULTIMATE PLAN FOR MAN

Those of us who grew up as excited Christians in the '60s and '70s were frequently encouraged and stimulated by teachings and books such as *The Late Great Planet Earth* by Hal Lindsay. Multitudes came to Christ through the preaching and message of the soon return of the Lord Jesus to the earth. The Jesus People Revival was in full swing, and the Lord's return was one of the foundational messages. Even Kathryn Kuhlman touched on the topic from time to time, and she led the greatest healing evangelistic meetings I had ever witnessed.

Political unrest on the earth at that time was also a contributing factor to the popularity of this message. There was much tension in the world because of the Cold War with Russia. The disillusionment of the Vietnam War was hugely impacting, and resistance and pushback were destabilizing America as young people tried to find a better solution. As time wore on, many Christian teachers armed with charts and Bible verses set dates by their speculations on when the Lord would return. I remember the book *88 Reasons Why Christ Will Return in 1988*. And then came its sequel, *89 Reasons Why the Rapture Will Be in 1989*.

That's what did it for me. I dropped the subject and focused on building the Church and extending the Kingdom through signs and wonders. Let's reach the lost, build the Church, and leave the return of the Lord to the Lord and His perfect timing. The whole topic went right off my radar. Carol and I were busy planting our churches, first in Stratford and then in Toronto, Ontario, and that turned out to be more than enough to keep us super busy.

And then January 20, 1994 happened! Revival exploded among us as the Holy Spirit came like a contagious, raging fire. We were suddenly catapulted into overwhelming crowds of spiritually hungry people who came to us from all parts of the globe and returned home on fire for God and raving about their divine encounter in Toronto. We were submerged in God's Glory while at the same time surrounded by challenging controversy over the intensity of the encounters and the reactive, stinging words of the naysayers who did not believe it could possibly be God at work.

I spent many years and many teachings presenting biblically based apologetics to defend what God was doing among us. The Glory remains to this present day as God continues to bless, heal, and restore through divine encounters. The godly fruit of these hundreds and thousands of life-changing immersions in Glory is a tremendous testimony to the life-transforming blessing and filling of the Holy Spirit. It is fulfilling the promise of the Father (see Acts 1:4-5). All is accomplished in the name and power of Jesus.

All of us need to realize that this global awakening is going somewhere. It is moving us forward toward our ultimate goal, the greatest event since Creation—global harvest and the return of the Lord Jesus Christ to earth! Surely it is time once again to talk about this hope-filled, life-giving message that is so near and dear to the heart of our Lord.

But where is the promise of His coming?

What about the great hope of the Church—the return of the Lord Jesus?

God tells us that scoffers will come in the last days with scoffing, following their own sinful desires:

> *They will say, "Where is the promise of his coming?*
> *For ever since the fathers fell asleep, all things are*
> *continuing as they were from the beginning of creation"*
> (2 Peter 3:4 ESV).

This begs the question, why is it taking so long? Skip down to verse nine:

> *The Lord is not slow to fulfill His promise as some count*
> *slowness, but is patient toward you, not wishing that*
> *any should perish, but that all should reach repentance*
> (2 Peter 3:9 ESV).

The Lord has planned and engineered these last 2,000 years to give all of humanity adequate time to decide whether or not we will serve Him, whether or not we will surrender to Jesus, whether or not we will be faithful to the truth He has told us, and we get to decide those issues within our lifetimes. That's why it has taken so long.

He wants millions of people to choose Him. And when the time is right, He will return absolutely, for sure, no question about it! The plan has always been for Jesus to rule over this earth as King.

Peter points out in Second Peter 3:8 that one day with the Lord is like 1,000 years, and 1,000 years is like a day. If we think a lifetime is a long time, 1,000 years is *really* long. How do we even relate to that?

Well, I've worked out that we need to be about 50 years old before we realize something very basic: Life is *short!* If you are over 50, do you remember your 50th birthday? My birthday is in the winter. When I turned 50, Carol gave me a surprise. I woke up to 50 pink flamingos all over our front lawn. There they all were. It was Christmas Day, and, oh my, how they all stood out, bright pink against the white, snow-covered lawn!

"Really, Carol?"

"*Yes!* Happy birthday, honey!"

When you first turn 50, you don't want to be reminded that you're now 50. Isn't that right? And then 60, of course. And 70. And you realize more and more that life really is short.

I remember my dad telling me, "Life is short, son." I was about 17 at the time. I thought, *Yeah, maybe for you. I've got my whole life ahead of me here.* You suddenly realize, *I'm 30, 50, 65, 70* and you are asking, "How did I get here?"

I turned 80 on Christmas 2020, and I can't deny it—80 is old. But then I started to think about it. How old is old when you're going to live forever? It's all just part of what God has set up for us while here on earth to see if we're going to do life His way or our own way. That's really the long and the short of it. (No pun intended.)

This message of the soon return of the Lord Jesus is actually vitally important because we really need to be ready for this climactic event. I'm genuinely concerned because most charismatic churches—our kind of churches—are not even talking about it anymore. Why on earth not?

There are some good reasons. We got burned out as time and time again people who set dates were wrong, and believers were ridiculed for it. There is much confusion among theologians as to how it will all work out—pre-trib, mid-trib, post-trib, or no-trib—and so we began to avoid this most important topic in Scripture. But we are fast coming up on this event, the greatest event in all of earth's history next to Creation itself—the return of King Jesus to rule and reign on the earth.

Now to make this a bit easier to follow, I believe Jesus' return is actually to take place in two parts:

- Part A: when He returns for His Bride, the Church, secretly.

- Part B: when He returns with His Bride very publicly, to rule and reign on earth.

If you read passages concerning His return and don't know the distinction between His secret return and His public return, you wonder which one it is. Is it secret or public? Does everyone see Him, or does nobody see Him? You have to know this distinction, but more about that later.

Now, let's look at Daniel 2. Daniel was a Judean captive in Babylon at the time when King Nebuchadnezzar ruled the empire. The king had a dream he couldn't understand, but he was wise. He thought, *If I tell those wise men* (his cadre of soothsayers and prophets) *my dream and ask for an interpretation, they will come up with something. I don't want them just to come up with "something," I want to know the real, true meaning of this dream.*

So he said to them, "Tell me the dream, and then tell me what it means."

They all freaked out: "That's impossible, your Majesty!"

"All right then, if you can't do it—guards, kill them all!"

Daniel came to the rescue: "Give me a couple of days to pray about it and see what God says."

The king agreed, and God answered. Look what happened:

> *There is a God in heaven who reveals mysteries, and he
> has made known to King Nebuchadnezzar what will be
> in the latter days* (Daniel 2:28 ESV).

Note what's going to come in the end times:

> *Your dream, and the visions in your head as you lay
> in bed are these: To you, O king, as you lay in bed
> came thoughts of what would be after this, and he
> who reveals mysteries made known to you what is
> to be* (Daniel 2:28-29 ESV).

Have you ever wondered what will be? What's coming? What is the end of this age? When is it going to happen? Read the Book of Revelation, get into the Word of God, and find out.

As you study the return of Jesus, you will find it is mentioned 29 times in the New Testament alone. *Epiphaneia* (appearing) is used five times, and *parousia* (arrival or coming) is used 24 times. Jesus referred many times to His coming, for example: *"When the Son of Man comes, will he find faith on earth?"* (Luke 18:8 ESV).

Jesus repeatedly referenced His return, and in the passage where Daniel tells the king what his royal highness had dreamed, God gives an outline of what was to transpire in history.

> *You saw, O king, and behold, a great image. This image, mighty and of exceeding brightness, stood before you, and its appearance was frightening. The head of this image was of fine gold, its chest and arms of silver, its middle and thighs of bronze, its legs of iron, its feet partly of iron and partly of clay. As you looked, a stone was cut out by no human hand, and it struck the image on its feet of iron and clay, and broke them in pieces. Then the iron, the clay, the bronze, the silver, and the gold, all together were broken in pieces, and became like the chaff of the summer threshing floors, and the wind carried them away, so that not a trace of them could be found. But the stone that struck the image became a great mountain and filled the whole earth* (Daniel 2:31-35 ESV).

Daniel goes on to interpret the dream to the king, saying (paraphrased), "You, O king, are the head of gold. Another kingdom inferior to yours shall arise after you—the Medes and the Persians who are represented by the arms of silver. Following them will come a king represented by a body of bronze."

Alexander the Great conquered the whole known world, and after his rule and that of his four generals ended came the Roman Empire in two parts. The legs of iron represented both the Western and Eastern Roman Empires. The Western Empire was ruled from the city of Rome, and the Eastern Empire from Constantinople, or the Byzantine Empire.

The Roman Empire lasted a very long time. Beginning circa 750 BC as a city state, it grew in power and influence, becoming an empire around 168 BC when it defeated the Greek Empire (331 BC to 168 BC). The eastern empire finally ended when Constantinople fell to the Turks on May 29, 1453. All in all, Rome lasted for more than 2,000 years before it eventually ended. For all those years, it was a strong political/military force with "legs of iron."

What came after the legs of iron? The feet of iron and clay. What do they stand for?

The feet of iron and clay speak of democracies. Iron symbolizes some of the remaining strength of the Roman Empire, but clay represents the common people. A democracy is therefore partly a strong system, but it is ruled by the populace, which makes it partly weak.

In the days of the kings or leaders who rule democracies—the time period we are in right now—we see both strengths and weaknesses. Have you noticed that lately? We see the weaknesses of democracies displayed before us all over the earth. They are appalling—front page news for all to debate following the morning news.

Doesn't it make you wonder what is going on? It helps to know we are in the days of the "kings" who rule democracies (see Dan. 2:34). Daniel said in those days (our days) a stone would be cut out of a mountain without hands, it would strike the world's system on its feet, and the whole thing would disintegrate totally. The democratic systems would become like the dust of a threshing floor and blow away, but that stone, the Lord Jesus, will grow and fill the whole earth:

> *In the days of those kings the God of heaven will set up a kingdom that shall never be destroyed, nor shall the kingdom be left to another people. It shall break in pieces all these kingdoms and bring them to an end, and it shall stand forever, just as you saw that a stone was cut from a mountain by no human hand, and that it broke in pieces the iron, the bronze, the clay, the silver, and the gold. A great God has made known to the king what shall be after this. The dream is certain, and its interpretation sure* (Daniel 2:44-45 ESV).

I love Daniel's comment: *"The dream is certain, and its interpretation sure"* (Dan. 2:45). This is really about to happen very soon, friend! Get ready!

We just reviewed an outline of history covering the last 2,600 years, which included Babylon! During this period the world saw the culmination of seven empires that interacted powerfully with Israel and also interfered with her. Since Egypt and Assyria had already come and

27

gone by Daniel's time, we were left with these remaining five: Babylon, Medes, and Persians, Greeks, Western and Eastern Rome, and now the democracies. Then comes their end and a new beginning with King Jesus ruling the earth from Jerusalem on the throne of David.

Lucky you! You're here at the time of the end!

Wow! This is so amazing, isn't it?

You see how this overview brings us to the hope of His return, which like I said will transpire in two parts. This is how I see biblical history, and it's the only perspective that makes the many prophetic Scriptures fit together in a way we can understand.

Do we have to work out the exact eschatology? I don't think anybody has it worked it out perfectly—not me, not you, not any of us—but we can come close. The main point is that we really need to be ready.

Are you ready?

Is it okay with you if Jesus returns?

Soon?

You see, it's on His heart to return, and He is coming back when He thinks it's right, not necessarily when you expect or whether or not you agree. So just settle that one. Jesus is most anxious for His Bride, the Church. I want Him to return as soon as He thinks everything is ready, whether or not I agree.

That's the unique thing about absolute ruling kings. They do things their way. They don't rule democratically, and democracies will pass away. Once we get to Heaven, you don't get to vote on stuff. That might be a shock to North Americans and Europeans: *What? Nobody asked me my opinion?*

No. The ruling was just handed down by the King who decided that's what He wants to do. But He's such a loving King! He has your best interests at heart. That's the great hope of His coming. So, when will that be?

2

BRING HOME YOUR BRIDE

First, He's coming secretly like a thief in the night for His Bride. Jesus' relationship with the Church, His Bride, parallels Jewish wedding patterns and customs. Study them.

Christie Eisner, a woman from Kansas City, has laid out the relationship between Jewish weddings and the Bride of Christ in a book entitled *Watching and Waiting: Encountering Jesus in the Fall Feasts,* and also in her first book, *Finding the Afikoman.* I'll come back to it when we discuss Matthew 25, but the New Testament follows this plan.

According to the pattern of Jewish weddings, the engagement was formal and legally binding. It was the first part of the marriage covenant. The groom-to-be and his parents would visit the bride's house and make the "deal." Once they covenanted together, they sealed the transaction by drinking wine, signing a document, and paying the bride price to the family and giving gifts to the bride, with a promise to return for her soon. The betrothal was now official. The bridegroom went home and built a house for his bride that was attached to his father's—a nice apartment. When it was ready, his father would say, "You're good to go. Go get your bride and bring her home!"

The groom gathered his friends, and making a lot of festive noise together, they went over the hill to the bride's house. The time of the groom's coming would be unannounced. He might even come at midnight, but when the bride's household heard the party arriving, it erupted into a lot of excitement and shouting: *"The bridegroom is coming!"*

The bride's parents or servants woke her up, and she realized, *Oh my goodness! I've got to get up and look my best for my groom.*

He swept her up in his arms, and off they went. The wedding would begin as soon as he arrived home.

Do you know how long Jewish wedding celebrations lasted? Seven days! I wonder how long Jesus' wedding might be? Maybe seven years, with one day representing an entire year. Meanwhile, what will transpire on the earth during that time?

> *But we do not want you to be uninformed, brothers, about those who are asleep, that you may not grieve as others do who have no hope. For since we believe that Jesus died and rose again, even so, through Jesus, God will bring with him those who have fallen asleep* (1 Thessalonians 4:13-14 ESV).

It appears the Thessalonian church was troubled by their lack of knowledge concerning Jesus' return. They seemed to be asking, "Has the Lord already come secretly, and we didn't know about it? How could that be, because people are dying off and we thought Jesus was coming back any moment? So what's going on?"

They were worried that maybe they had missed His return. Paul reassured them, "No, no! It's okay."

He settled them down and then taught them:

> *For this we declare to you by a word from the Lord,*
> *that we who are alive, who are left* [Paul included
> himself in that number] *until the coming of the*
> *Lord, will not precede those who have fallen asleep. For*
> *the Lord himself will descend from heaven with a cry of*
> *command, with the voice of an archangel, and with the*
> *sound of the trumpet of God. And the dead in Christ*
> *will rise first. Then we who are alive, who are left, will*
> *be caught up* [harpazo] *together with them in the*
> *clouds to meet the Lord in the air, and so we will always*
> *be with the Lord. Therefore encourage one another with*
> *these words* (1 Thessalonians 4:15-18 ESV).

Did you hear what that verse just said? Encourage or comfort one another with these words. The Greek word used here is *parakaleite*, the same word used to describe the Comforter, the Holy Spirit. This event alone should bring great joy and comfort to all who love His appearing. So let's think about this again for a minute.

The dead in Christ are going to rise first. How many dead Christians do you think there are throughout the last

34

2,000 years? Just a wild guess. Half a billion? Five hundred million, maybe? And that number might be low.

How many living Christians are there who are excited about the Lord's return? We are speaking of the whole world here. Think about it—there's China, India, Australia, New Zealand, Latin America, North America, Europe, Africa, and the Middle East.

Do you think there might be another half a billion people in that worldwide group? I would say minimally so. If all those people go up in the Rapture, we are talking about a cataclysmic event. It will be the most exciting, earth-shaking event you can possibly imagine. A half billion people will come out of their graves in glorified bodies first, including your beloved Christian grandparents and your Christian friend who died too soon. Then you and I, who are still in these bodies, will be changed and transformed in a moment—in a flash. Is that not beyond our comprehension? But this is the clear teaching of Scripture! Yet if you talk to people about it, they may look at you dumbfounded:

"Do you really believe this?"

"Uh-huh! I do."

"Based on what?"

"Based on the fact that my Savior was crucified, died, was buried, and in three days rose again supernaturally, being the first to be raised from the dead."

3

FIRST FRUITS FULFILLED

You know what happened when Jesus rose? A whole bunch of others rose with Him (see Matt. 27:52-53). Who were those people? Would it have been Abraham, David, or Moses? Perhaps, but I think they may have been followers of Jesus who died during His earthly ministry. In the three and a half years of His earthly ministry some people would have died, because thousands followed Him. When they rose from the dead, their graves were opened, and people in Jerusalem marveled:

"Hey look! The graves opened, and we saw people we knew who had died. Remember old Zeke? Well, he came back resurrected, and he was walking around downtown!"

This event was a perfect fulfillment of the Feast of the Passover. The Feast of the Passover has three elements:

- The Passover lamb was sacrificed.

- Unleavened bread only was eaten.

- The Feast of First Fruits was the first day after the actual Sabbath.

If we count 50 days forward from the Feast of the First Fruits, we arrive at the date of the Feast of Pentecost. What is the significance of the Feast of First Fruits?

Back in the day, the priests went into the barley fields when the grain was barely ripening and picked whatever number of prematurely ripened heads of grain they could gather. They brought the handful back to the Temple and waved it before the Lord on the first day after Shabbat during this Feast of Passover/Unleavened Bread. While the priests in Israel were gathering that little symbol, saying, "The harvest is coming," and waving it before the Lord as a Feast of First Fruits offering, Heaven was fulfilling that prophetic act at the same time as Jesus rose from the dead and others rose and then ascended with Him.

That is the significance of the wave offering before the Lord. He rose, and He is about to return. Do you know why? Because that stone *will* be cut out of the mountain; the Savior will be cut out of humanity (born of a woman), and He *will* strike a finishing blow to the kingdoms of this world. Democracies and the whole world's system will collapse, according to Daniel's night vision and revelation from Daniel 2:35, 44, and 45. It'll be a *new world order* all right—God's divine order with King Jesus on His glorious throne, ruling and reigning as earth's King of kings. What a fantastic future we have!

That is why it says in First Thessalonians 4:18, *"Therefore encourage* [or comfort] *one another with these words."* We need to read this passage carefully with hope and excitement for our future:

> *Then we who are alive, who are left, will be caught*
> *up together with them in the clouds to meet the Lord*
> *in the air, and so we will always be with the Lord*
> (1 Thessalonians 4:17 ESV).

Say "caught up" to yourself.

People will tell you that the word *rapture* is not in the Bible. Have you heard that? Do you know that's not true?

Rapture is a Latin word, so it absolutely appears in the Latin Bible, but in the Greek language, the original language of our New Testament, the word used is *harpazo*. Do you know what it means? Caught up! Do a word study on *harpazo* for your own interest. It's used 14 times in the New Testament, and it means to be snatched or grabbed suddenly. One minute you are doing your thing, and the next minute you are gone. That's the word the writer of the Book of Acts used to describe what happened to Philip (see Acts 8:26-40) when he met up with the Ethiopian and explained the Scripture concerning Jesus to him. The eunuch said, "Hey, there's some water. Let me be baptized there."

After Philip baptized him, Scripture says the Spirit of the Lord caught him away—*harpazo!* What a glorious encounter he had with the Holy Spirit! He flew through the air to the coast, about 30 miles away from where he met the eunuch. Philip was supernaturally transported. That's amazing!

How would you like to travel that way? It is within our potential, especially with what's coming.

Thus *harpazo* is the Greek word for "rapture," but it signifies being grabbed or snatched away suddenly.

> *Then we who are alive and remain shall be **caught up** together with them in the clouds to meet the Lord in the air* (1 Thessalonians 4:17 ESV).

Where will this meeting be? In the air, in the clouds. Let's cross-reference that with one of my favorite chapters in Scripture, John 14. Here Jesus was telling His disciples, "Hey guys, don't be upset. I have to go away."

The disciples wondered: *Why would that be upsetting to us? We're all in. We left our businesses, left everything...*

I love how calm and cool Jesus is all the time—just like you would expect the Messiah to be. He continued, "Where I'm going you can't follow Me now, but you will follow Me later on."

The disciples were bewildered. *What? I thought He was the Messiah! How can He be leaving now? The job is not finished.*

How can He deliver Israel from the Romans if He's gone? What is He talking about now?

Later, they were in shock when Jesus was arrested. They likely thought, *He'll break out, and all those soldiers will fall at His feet.*

But that didn't happen. They would watch Him die, but He coached them through the process:

> *Let not your hearts be troubled. Believe in God; believe also in me. In my Father's house are many rooms. If it were not so, would I have told you that I go to prepare a place for you?* (John 14:1-2 ESV)

4

HEAVEN COMES FIRST

Just like the Jewish bridegroom, He made a deal with them, saying He would go away to get their house ready:

> *And if I go and prepare a place for you, I will come again and will take you to myself, that where I am you may be also* (John 14:3 ESV).

Well, wait a minute! What about you? Where will you be going when He comes back to get you? You won't be on earth any longer, but you will be with Him in Heaven. You'll be going to the place He has prepared. People often get confused. Are we going to Heaven up in the sky, or is Heaven going to be on earth? We are going to be in both places, actually, but in Heaven first.

You see, there is going to be a wedding in Heaven first. Jesus went to Heaven where He's preparing a place for you. That's why He said, "I am going to receive you unto Myself so that where I am there you may be also." Do you want to go there?

A good book you need to read is called *Imagine Heaven* by John Burke. It tells dozens of stories about people who have had "near-death experiences" and who have seen into a dimension beyond our own. Have you read books about life after death? Not only do Christians believe there is life after death, but so do New Agers and people from other religions. In this case, pastor John Burke wrote this book to compare people's experiences for consistency. Prior to writing *Imagine Heaven*, he examined about 1,000 accounts of people who had died and were resuscitated. They were communists, atheists, Muslims, Hindus, Jews, and others, as well as Christians. His findings were very informative.

All the people he studied saw the same sorts of things. He was able to cross-reference their experiences to Scripture and found they were biblical. He said the problem was not with what they had seen and experienced but how they interpreted their stories when they returned to earth.

Another issue was that of credibility. For instance, someone might have come back from a near-death experience and told their story in church: "I just went to Heaven, and Jesus was there. All I could feel was this incredible love from Him."

The person's family and friends may have responded, "Well, that couldn't be from God, because if anybody deserved God's condemnation it's you."

People such as these—precious living witnesses of the life beyond—can often be quickly marginalized by telling their story to believers. Instead of finding acceptance among believers, they subsequently find it in a New Age group. Isn't that sad? As I read this book to Carol, I realized we know two of the people mentioned in this book: Steve Sjogren from Cincinnati, Ohio, and Ian McCormack who's in New Zealand. What incredible stories they tell.

We recorded an interview with Ian, and he said, "John, I didn't have a near-death experience. I died. I was dead for 40 minutes and then came back, because the Lord said, 'It's not your time.'"

Go to our website, johnandcarol.org, look under Events, and then Archives. Search for Ian McCormack.[1] It's worth hearing his full story, because he really told it all when we interviewed him. The Steve Sjogren and John Burke interviews are there as well.[2]

Ian shared how real and beautiful Heaven is, and how incredibly loving God was toward him. In the interview he recalled, "I was in a very dark place and demons were jeering at me. It was really bad, dark, and it got darker. In the darkness I looked up and I saw a very, very tiny little light, so I cried out, 'Jesus, help me!' When I said that, the light just sped down toward me and opened up into a tunnel. Whoosh! I was sucked up through that tunnel of light."

He flew out of the darkness and found himself standing in the presence of the Lord. There was Jesus! "He was looking at me, and all I felt was incredible love pouring into me."

"Where am I?" Ian asked the Lord.

"You're in Heaven, Ian."

Unexpectedly, Ian was dismayed. "Oh no!" he cried. "Someone's made a terrible mistake. I don't deserve to be here."

Again, he felt a whoosh of great love, but still he was convinced he shouldn't be in Heaven. "No!" he said to Jesus. "Surely You know the terrible things I've done in my life." He began confessing his sins—I've done this, I've done that—but he just kept feeling more and more love pouring into him. Eventually he said, "I don't understand."

Then the Lord spoke. "When you prayed the Lord's prayer with your dying breath, you said, 'Forgive me of my sins as I forgive those who have sinned against me.' You forgave those who sinned against you, and I forgave you for all your sins. So there is absolutely nothing now between you and Me." Ian said he dissolved into tears.

Ian's is such a great story about our future home. This, my friend, is where we're going. When you're 50 and you start to figure out that life is short, hopefully you start to think about what comes afterward. It is amazing to realize that most people don't ever want to talk about death or what comes after that. They're happy to postpone that conversation forever. But consider this:

I have friends who went on vacation to Albania. They were excited about going to a country where they had never been before, so they went online and researched everything about it—the mountains in the north, the beaches in the south, the cities, the country, the people, the language, the food—everything. They wanted to know about their destination as much as possible so they could enjoy it even more once they got there. Don't you think it's reasonable to do the same thing concerning your next life? Once you come out of your body, where are you going to go?

Notes

1. Catch the Fire Ministries, http://www.johnandcarol.org/ eventhistory/july-1st-interview-with-ian-mccormack.

2. Catch the Fire Ministries, http://www.johnandcarol.org/ eventhistory/june-3rd-at-home-with-john-and-carol -imagine-heaven-with-john-burke.

5

HARVEST IS
HAPPENING *NOW*

People are afraid of death. That is one of the reasons many turn to Jesus. He is the only one who has the words of eternal life (see John 6:68). Do you know God has used COVID-19 to cause many people to think about eternal things? Recently I talked to Ron, a casual friend who has missions in several parts of the world. He told me that fear of COVID is driving people to accept Christ like nothing he's ever seen before.

Another reason people come to know Jesus is through God's sovereign intervention. In Ethiopia, where there is a tremendous revival, Ron learned of many Muslims who have come to faith in Christ. He asked a large group of his leaders and new believers, "How many of your Islamic leaders and imams have had a dream or a vision of the Man in White?" The men huddled together and talked about it in their own language a few minutes and came back to him with an answer. "We don't know of any Muslim leader who has not had a dream or seen a vision of the Man in White." Jesus is appearing supernaturally to so many all over the globe.

You see, the Lord is not limited to our attempts to evangelize. They haven't worked all that effectively for us, but of course we must keep going. Yet God Himself evangelizes as well, so much more effectively. We are hearing many stories of entire Muslim villages having the same dream about the "Prophet Isa" (Jesus) coming to them and saying, "I am the way. Follow Me."

Can you imagine people in a village getting up in the morning and saying, "I had an amazing dream last night," and their friends replying, "That's exactly the same dream I had!"

They talk and find out half the village has had that same dream.

When the Lord is ready to harvest the earth, I'm telling you, the harvest is on! He said, *"I will come again and will take you to myself"* (John 14:3).

6

ANCIENT PROPHECIES
SPECTACULARLY FULFILLED

Let's now consider together some Scriptures that pertain to fulfilled prophecy. Here's a question for you: When we read the following Scripture verses today, how are they different for us than they were for someone reading them 1,000 years ago? In the year AD 1022 people puzzled over Matthew 24, Luke 21, and Mark 13. They might have asked, "What do these chapters mean?"

They tried to figure out the passages. They sought God: "Lord, when is Your coming? Where is the promise of You coming?"

What if someone had said, "Don't worry about it. Jesus' return is around 1,000 years away"?

Imagine the bewilderment. "But these Scriptures say He could return *now*—any moment."

It has been that way throughout time—through history. The Holy Spirit inspired these passages to be written in such a way that every generation honestly thought Jesus' return would be imminent. My grandfather thought he would be alive when Jesus returned, but it didn't happen. Someday, however, some of us will see it. Would you like to be one of those people? It would be nice to skip the "dying" part and leave to meet the Lord in the air in "a twinkling of an eye," wouldn't it? I am up for that totally.

There are at least three very important differences in the way we perceive these particular Scriptures today and the way our forefathers understood them. Let's look at them:

1. The Nation of Israel

Do you know why so many of the mainline churches believe in replacement theology? It goes all the way back to Origen, one of the early church fathers. Origen was a third-century theologian originally from Alexandria.

In his day there had been such a mighty move of God that almost the whole Roman Empire had converted to Christianity. The promise of a great falling away seemed to have been replaced by successful global evangelism. They thought that perhaps the prophetic Scriptures needed to be interpreted differently as well—allegorically rather than literally.

On what teaching should the Church focus once the entire city was won to Christ?

What could the theological focus be for raising children in the ways of God?

There was a need to hold and maintain the ground that had been taken now that the Roman Empire itself had become Christian (the Byzantines).

Origen began to think about the promises God made to Israel that one day it would become a nation again. He wondered if the promises could be metaphors referring to the Church, and he began spiritualizing them and allegorizing them. His point of view caught on.

Augustine took Origen's work to a new level, and his perspective became the accepted standard for the Orthodox and the Catholic Churches. The Reformation didn't touch this eschatological point of view, and thus it remained embedded in the belief system of the Church in general. But God's promises in Bible passages such as Ezekiel 36 are still very clearly for Israel to anyone who reads them. The whole chapter records God saying, "I'll restore you again and bring you into your own land" (see Ezek. 36:22-24).

Do you know the land of Israel was promised to the Jewish people three times? First through Abraham, then through Isaac, and then through Jacob. None of them got the land, but they lived in it until they went to Egypt. They were delivered from slavery in Egypt 400 years later when God brought them back into the land of Israel supernaturally with Moses and Joshua as their leaders. Later they were conquered by the Assyrians and the Babylonians. Then their investment in the land was wiped out, the temple was burned, and the people were conquered.

Seventy years later, according to the prophecy of Jeremiah, they were again supernaturally brought back to the land (see Jer. 29:10). Isn't that amazing? As Daniel read Jeremiah's book, he began praying into the 70-year prophecy and subsequently had a visit from the angel Gabriel. It's an incredible passage of Scripture, because the angel Gabriel told Daniel exactly when the Messiah would come and then be killed. In Daniel 9 we read how many weeks of years would be involved.

Sir Robert Anderson, who was the head of Scotland Yard and a devout Christian, published a book in 1894 titled *The Coming Prince.* He worked out the math concerning the 69-week prophecy of Daniel 9.

> *Know therefore and understand that from the going forth of the command* [by Artaxerxes Longimanus] *to restore and build Jerusalem* [not the Temple, but the city] *until Messiah the Prince, there shall be seven weeks and sixty-two weeks* [69 weeks of years]; *the street shall be built again, and the wall, even in troublesome times* (Daniel 9:25).

It works out exactly to the day when Jesus rode in on the donkey proclaiming Himself King. Right to the *day!*

If you acquire Sir Robert Anderson's book (the eBook is on Amazon Kindle), you can check the math. The answers are there if you're willing to do a bit of digging. Don't just believe all the sceptics out there spiritualizing God's Word. His Word will be fulfilled to the dotting of every "i" and the crossing of every "t." Make no mistake about it!

Ezekiel 36 and 37 speak of the return of the Jews to Israel and the valley of dry bones, which is the whole House of Israel. The "bones" of the House of Israel are very dry. "Prophesy to them," said the Lord. "Tell them to come alive" (see Ezek. 37:12). This text is prophetic in terms of predicting that Israel would come alive again, which it did on May 14, 1948.

Read Isaiah 49. It proclaims the restoration of Israel. The Land was promised first to Abraham, Isaac, and Jacob, and that promise was fulfilled under Moses and Joshua. Israel was restored again under Nehemiah and Ezra after Israel's Babylonian captivity, and then restored a final time in 1948.

I was a little boy, seven years old, when Israel became a nation again 1,878 years after Rome destroyed it in AD 70. Get this—it was restored to have:

- the same ancient land

- the same ancient language

- the same ancient religion

That has never happened to any other group of people throughout all of history. The others were conquered and assimilated within the cultures of the conquerors. That's how it works. But Israel was somehow supernaturally preserved, and even their Hebrew language was resurrected. An absolutely amazing fulfillment of prophecy! After all those years! How many years again? *One thousand eight hundred and seventy-eight!*

The second Scripture to consider is Luke 21:24, a prophecy of Jesus.

2. The Time of the Gentiles

Jerusalem would be under the control of the Gentiles (the Nations) until the time of the Gentiles would be fulfilled. This is an ominous word.

I was in Bible school in 1967 when the Six-day War broke out and I was glued to the TV. *Oh my gosh!* I thought. *What's going to happen?* And then, the war was over in six days. I couldn't believe it! *Who can win and end a war in six days? Are you serious? Six days?*

Not only that, but Israel also took all the territories: Sinai, Gaza, the Golan Heights, the West Bank—they took everything in six days. It had to be God. Jerusalem was totally recovered—all of it, including the Temple Mount. It is now entirely in Jewish hands. They have allowed the Arabs to manage it, but when issues arise, the Israeli police control access. Have you been up there? It is a most interesting hot spot.

3. The Gospel of the Kingdom

According to Matthew 24:14, the Gospel of the Kingdom must go out to the entire world—also a prophecy of Jesus. The Gospel will be preached in all the world as a witness to the nations, and then the end will come. This is the third time marker. All three of these are timestamps:

When did Israel become a nation? 1948.

When was Jerusalem taken again? 1967.

Has the Gospel been preached in every nation? Yes.

Every nation has heard the message of the Kingdom today. It isn't necessary to smuggle Bibles into China, Iran, or elsewhere any longer because people can simply download their favorite Bible on their phones. Just like that! The Church is in every nation around the world right now, and every Gospel program is available to the whole world via the internet and live streaming. Now clearly, not every individual has heard, and there are remote tribes and people groups who still have no Bible, or even no New Testaments in their own mother tongue. But most of these people do have access using one of the main languages of their nation. The good news is that there are Christians and churches in every nation, and the Bible, or at least parts of the New Testament, is available in all the world's main languages.

What a day we live in! How amazing it is!

This Gospel of the Kingdom will penetrate and impact the entire world, and then the end will come. A believer communicating with the Lord at the time of the disciples might have asked, "What, Lord? We're going to proliferate and spread this good news all over the world? Why?"

"Because I'm taking over and that's what I want you to do."

"Oh. Okay, how long will it take?"

"A couple thousand years (couple of days) and then the end will come."

I want to conclude these thoughts with the *prophetic parable of the fig tree.*

The fig tree is a type of Israel. The dream of every Israeli leaving Egypt circa 1500 BC was to sit one day under his own grape vine and his own fig tree and be free to raise his own family on his own farm.

According to Jeremiah, the fig tree symbolizes Israel (see Jer. 24:1-10). He saw two baskets of figs—one was rotten and the other good. The Lord told him they represented the House of Israel.

Consider the following in light of the fact that figs and therefore fig trees are symbols for Israel.

Do you remember reading how Jesus cursed the fig tree in His last few days in Jerusalem (see Matt. 21:19)? Picture it:

"I'm feeling hungry. I see a fig tree over there. I wonder if there are any figs on it? Hmmm! Nothing but leaves! I curse you, fig tree! Never again are you going to bear fruit!"

Come on, Jesus, that's not like You!

It just seems so out of character for Jesus to act that way. Have you ever wondered what that was all about? I wondered about it for years until I got the answer.

The fig tree is a type of Israel, so when Jesus spoke to the fig tree, He was speaking to Israel in type and symbol. Here's what He was saying:

Israel, you produce nothing but "leaves," and you will never produce "food" again. If anybody wants the fruit of Heaven, they will need to come through the Savior Jesus Christ Himself. From now on, He is the only way into God's Kingdom. The Law will no longer produce fruit.

Israel is the fig tree, and Jesus' prophecy turned out to be a one-generation prophecy. It is recorded in Matthew and Luke. Let's look at the one in Matthew 24.

From the fig tree learn its lesson: as soon as its branch becomes tender and puts out its leaves, you know that summer is near. So also, when you see all these things, you know that he is near, at the very gates. Truly, I say to you, this generation will not pass away until all these things take place. Heaven and earth will pass away, but my words will not pass away (Matthew 24:32-35 ESV).

Jesus spoke these words to people who heard Him, but His message could not have applied to them because they are now long gone. What generation was He talking to? He was speaking to the generation that sees the fig tree blossoming and putting fourth its leaves once again. He said, *"From the fig tree learn its lesson: as soon as its branch becomes tender and puts out its leaves, you know that summer is near"* (Matt. 24:32 ESV). What does that mean?

Summer to us means a beach vacation, holidays, and warmer weather, but to multiple millions throughout history, summer has meant harvest time. *Harvest time!*

In other words, when you see Israel become a nation, you'll know harvest time is coming, and His return is very near. Jesus is very clear with this message.

He said we would see:

- Israel become a nation—the Fig Tree is alive again and sprouting as of 1948.

- Jerusalem, including the old city, become a Jewish city again—fulfilled in 1967.

- The Gospel preached around the world— almost there.

He also indicated we should see the things that will characterize the end of the age (see Matt. 24:4-33; Luke 21:8-36). When we see these things, we know His coming is "right at the gate."

Jesus then doubled down on this message of the fig tree. He emphasized, *"this generation will not pass away until all these things take place. Heaven and earth will pass away, but my words will not pass away"* (Matt. 24:34-35 ESV).

The things Jesus prophesied are going to happen, and we're at the gate of His coming right now. This is a one-generation prophecy, to be fulfilled within one generation. Some of the generation of 1948 will still be around—the ones who saw the Fig Tree sprouting its leaves. They will not completely pass away until all of these things are fulfilled. His return is so close!

You may live to be 90, but in the Bible it says a person's life is about 70 years. According to Psalm 90:10, 70 years is about what you get, more or less, all things considered. Hopefully you can count on that, but if you are really strong, you can make it up to, or perhaps over 80 years. I take it then that some people alive will perhaps be 80-plus years old, or perhaps even 90 when the Lord's return is complete.

"All these things being fulfilled"—that would put the return of the Lord roughly around 2028 to 2038, which is just a few years away now. If you deduct seven years for the royal wedding of Jesus and His Bride, that could mean the Rapture and Jesus' return for His Bride would be seven years before the actual return to establish His Kingdom on earth.

Another passage that ties into this thought is found in Joel 3:1-2:

> *For behold, in those days and at that time, when I*
> *restore the fortunes of Judah and Jerusalem, I will*
> *gather all the nations and bring them down to the*
> *Valley of Jehoshaphat. And I will enter into judgment*
> *with them there, on behalf of my people and my*
> *heritage Israel, because they have scattered them*
> *among the nations and have divided up my land.*
> (Joel 3:1-2 ESV)

This is another one generation prophecy which tells us that at the time and season that Israel is restored, the final judgment will take place in the Valley of Jehoshaphat (Kidron Valley) outside of Jerusalem.

7

A ROYAL WEDDING INDEED

Concerning the wedding, Matthew says, *"The kingdom of heaven may be compared to a king who gave a wedding feast for his son"* (Matt. 22:2 ESV).

When the Toronto revival first fell on us in January 1994, my wife Carol had a powerful vision. It was probably the most powerful one she has ever had. When the vision came, she was on the platform to receive prayer because we were about to go on a mission. While our team was praying for Carol, she was taken away in the Spirit. She lay on the platform making a lot of noise, stomping and yelling and being very distracting. She was just "gone"!

Mark Dupont was preaching that day, and she was such a distraction. Her legs were up in the air, and she was running, shouting, and obviously having a divine encounter. (See Carol's recent book *The Spirit and the Bride Say "Come!"*) Someone came to me and whispered, "Should we remove Carol from the platform?"

"Nobody touch her!" I said. "She wouldn't do that for a million dollars. This is God, and we aren't disturbing her. Leave her alone."

Carol was on the floor like that for 40 minutes or so. Later, when the supernatural experience subsided, she told us she had had a beautiful vision of being in a meadow with Jesus. They danced together, and then arm in arm they walked on streets of gold. Jesus took her into a glorious banquet hall that went on as far as the eye could see. It was filled with tables set with silverware and crystal, all beautifully decorated. Carol asked Jesus, "Who are all these beautiful people?"

"These are the poor, the unwanted, the destitute, and the ones nobody cares for, and I have bidden them to come to My banquet."

Carol marveled at the scene. "Wow, this is so beautiful. What do You want me to do with this, Lord?"

"Get up and tell My people that the banquet feast is almost prepared. You are to be like the five wise virgins who have extra oil, for now is the time to buy oil."

Carol scrambled out of the vision, jumped to her feet, and blurted out Jesus' message. We were awestruck! We had never personally known anyone who had a vision like that.

Carol's experience deposited something in my heart, and I wanted to glean everything that God had to say about this. I must have studied that passage of Matthew 25 fifty times or more. Let's read it together now:

> *Then the kingdom of heaven will be like ten virgins who took their lamps and went to meet the bridegroom. Five of them were foolish, and five were wise. For when the foolish took their lamps, they took no oil with them, but the wise took flasks of oil with their lamps. As the bridegroom was delayed, they all became drowsy and slept* (Matthew 25:1-5 ESV).

"What about us?" I asked the Father. "Couldn't we say the Bridegroom has been delayed about 2,000 years?" I read it, and read it, and read it, and one day I read verse 5 where it says they all slumbered and slept. I said, "God, I don't feel like I'm asleep. We're in the midst of revival. People are coming from all the nations—from all over the world. Planeloads of people are getting saved, healed, and filled with the Holy Spirit. I don't feel like I'm asleep. These are the best days of my life and ministry."

Then, like lightning God answered me: "You are asleep concerning the message of the soon return of the Lord Jesus Christ!"

The words were like a spear that went through me, and I realized, *Oh my gosh! I haven't preached this message for at least ten years!* Why? Because I got disillusioned. So many have predicted dates and their speculations turned out to be wrong. Others had such diverse but strong opinions about how it will transpire, so I just laid it all aside, saying, "Lord, come when You want to come. I will get busy and disciple Christians and hopefully win the lost." But now I feel such an urgency to share this message. I said, "Oh, Lord God, help me! I want to get this right!"

The text goes on:

> *But at midnight there was a cry, "Here is the bridegroom! Come out to meet him." Then all those virgins rose and trimmed their lamps. And the foolish said to the wise, "Give us some of your oil, for our lamps are going out." But the wise answered, saying, "Since there will not be enough for us and for you, go rather to the dealers and buy for yourselves." And while they were going to buy, the bridegroom came, and those who were ready went in with him to the marriage feast, and the door was shut. Afterward the other virgins came also, saying, "Lord, lord, open to us." But he answered, "Truly, I say to you, I do not know you." Watch therefore, for you know neither the day nor the hour* (Matthew 25:6-13 ESV).

The takeaway is, five *virgins* got to go somewhere where the other five *virgins* did not get to go.

People have asked me, "Well, John, what do you believe about eschatology? Are you pre-trib or post-trib?" I say, "Actually I believe in both, but I want to be on the first flight out. I want to be with the wise guys—and have extra oil!"

Do you know what the oil refers to? It indicates intimacy with the Holy Spirit. This story is all about love and intimacy. It is a wedding paradigm. Such a rich word! The Gospel writer doesn't use the word *gnosco* when Jesus says, "I never knew you." Of course, Jesus knows all about you—your name, where you live, and so on. But here the writer uses the Greek word *oida*, literally meaning "to see." It means to be intimately acquainted with or know a person intimately rather than casually. This is a bridal passage after all, and Jesus is looking for a Bride that is absolutely in love with Him. This oil is the oil of intimacy. If someone is not intimate with Jesus through the Holy Spirit, Jesus might say to them:

I never saw you. You were never in the secret place with me. You were never "soaking" or just spending time with me. You were always so busy with your own interests and concerns.

Friends, we need to be buying oil now. Carol has a new book on soaking simply called *Soaking in the Spirit*. You need to get it. The days are upon us when Jesus could come suddenly for His Bride. The Bride is supposed to be someone who is absolutely in love with Him and not so worried about the cares of this life that she misses Him and what is important to Him.

I learned so much from Carol when we were dating. We were both from broken marriages. I had been so hurt by it that I vowed that no woman would ever hurt me like that again. Carol got through my defenses somehow, and I realized she was probably the only exception in the world—a woman I could trust. (I've since learned that there are many others.)

After dating for a couple of years and realizing that we were getting serious about each other, I said to her one day, "Carol, will you marry me?" I was waiting for her to be practical and say, "Well, we've got a lot to think about. First of all, you've got two girls; I've got two boys. We have no money. How is that going to work? Let me pray about it."

But she didn't do that at all. Instead, she said, *"Oh yes!"* And you know what? I couldn't believe what I was hearing!

We've been married now for more than 23 years, and what she said back then still blesses me to this day. I tell her that every now and then, but you see, that's what Jesus expects from you and me. He wants to know, "Will you marry me? Are you excited about it?"

Sometimes people are so non-committal: "Hmmm, well yeah, but let me think about it. What's in it for me? Do I need a marriage contract here?"

Jesus doesn't want any of that. He wants somebody who is absolutely in love with Him for all He is and for all He does. A commitment like that brings the very best life ever. It's based on love, not on practicality, or even on being mutually beneficial. He doesn't want a Bride who wants to marry Him for His money, but one who is deeply in love with Him and wants to spend eternity with Him.

We're coming down to the finish now, folks, down to the wire, and it's serious because five of the virgins from Matthew 25 didn't make it to the wedding. They realized too late what they were missing (the oil of intimacy) and Jesus said to them: *I never saw you. You were busy with yourself, wrapped up in your own life, your own needs and desires. You were not preoccupied with Me.*

I learned what being preoccupied means through my youngest granddaughter, Jackie, when she was getting married. Her wedding was all she could talk about.

"Honey, how is university going?"

"Uh, fine. But have you seen my website about wedding gifts?"

"Yeah, I saw that. How's your little part-time job doing?"

"Okay, but Papa, you are going to be at the wedding? You blocked out that date? You're coming for sure? Aren't you?"

She was preoccupied with her wedding, and she's just so happily married today. I said to myself, *I want to be like Jackie toward You, Jesus. I want to be so in love with You that nothing else matters—not really.*

Concerning this little bit of stuff we accumulate throughout life, let it all go. When He comes, I go. I will leave everything behind, because where we're going is so fantastic.

So where is the promise of His coming?

Do you know the Bible says in such an hour as you think *not* the Son of Man comes? What if it's today? What if it's next week? What would you do differently? If I was sure He was coming next week, I would pray like I've always wanted to pray. If you want to be one of those five wise virgins, wave your hands to Him.

> *Father, we sense that things are coming to a head right now in our day. Israel has been your nation for more than 73 years, and Jerusalem has been Your city for more than 54 years. **Maranatha, Lord!** This is how Your book ends: "Even so, come, Lord Jesus!"* (Rev. 22:20).

> *May we, Your people, fall freshly in love with You, Jesus, so we can get our hearts ready and prepared to be awakened suddenly one day when You come as our Bridegroom King, and we go out and up to meet You.*

> *May the embrace of the Lord Jesus Christ be with us! Amen.*

So yes, He is returning very soon, friend. If you believe in an eschatology that says Christians are going through the Great Tribulation (the time of God's wrath), then perhaps you misunderstand how the judgment of God is different from persecution by the world, the flesh, and the devil. They're not one and the same. Why would He say, "Comfort one another with these words," if we as believers are to go through the Tribulation?

Often people aren't excited about the second coming of Jesus because they have been persuaded that they're going through the time of trouble. Who can get excited about that? If you think you must go through the Tribulation, you're probably saying, "Don't come yet, Lord! We need to get our house paid off and our kids through college! We need to get this, that, and the other done first."

No, no! Wait a minute! No! He's the *Savior* of the world. Scripture says He's going to *rescue you* from God's wrath. Read it in Luke:

> *But stay awake at all times, praying that you may have strength to escape all these things that are going to take place, and to stand before the Son of Man* (Luke 21:36 ESV).

Wow! That's what I want to do!

I ask You, Lord, put that seed in every heart and send it out with the best message we could ever have: Jesus is coming soon, and it's going to be a great day and a great celebration for those who had the wisdom to acquire extra oil. Oh, I pray that extra oil flows upon you now, in Jesus' wonderful name. Amen.

8

BE NOT DECEIVED

What About Deception?

What do you think might be the foremost characteristic of the end times? Climate change? Human trafficking? Oppression of the Church? Depopulation? Financial collapse? Terrible wars?

These and many other issues of our time are catastrophic, but they didn't make it on Jesus' list of important end-time signs. In Matthew 24, that great chapter on end-time revelation when He addressed the end times, amazingly Jesus had a lot to say about an entirely different matter—deception, especially as it pertains to the last days and the end times.

I was surprised when I realized that among end-time signs, He warned us three times, *in Matthew 24 alone, not to be deceived.* Apparently, He considered it a very important matter.

Let's look at the things Jesus tells us about the end times in that chapter.

In a private conversation with the disciples (see Matt. 24:3), the disciples asked Him what would be the sign of His coming and of the end of the age. Jesus responded saying, *"Take heed that no one deceives you!"*

One might expect Him to point to an event or personality as a sign to watch for, yet He distinctly directed us to look out for deception and for those who intentionally try to deceive us. That indicates deception will be a major sign of the end times.

Additionally, of course, He lists:

- wars and rumors of wars

- nations opposing nations

- calamities such as famines, pestilences, and earthquakes

- signs in the sun and moon

These signs are just the beginning of earth's labor pains that bring on the end times, but in verse 11 He again says that many false prophets will arise and deceive many.

That is the second warning in this chapter about deception.

He goes on to mention other signs:

- Lawlessness will abound.

- The love of many will grow cold.

- Those who endure to the end will be saved.

From this Scripture we glean that we are to endure, persevere, and hold on to the orthodox and apostolic truths of our historical faith.

Then in verse 14, He declares:

- This Gospel of the Kingdom will be preached in all the world as a witness to all nations.

- Then the end will come.

The end comes once the entire world has had a comprehensive presentation of the Gospel of the Kingdom, as I believe it has pretty much had today. Every nation has heard, and there is a witnessing church in every country on earth. The internet is crammed full of Gospel presentations.

The third reference to deception points out that in the end times deception will be very strong and convincing. In verse 24 we read that false "christs" and false "prophets" will rise and show great signs and wonders to deceive, if possible, even the elect. The deception they propagate is accompanied by great signs and lying wonders so as to almost deceive the very elect—the sincerest Christians among us.

I hate that, by the way. Indeed, it would be a very strong deception.

I find it amazing that Jesus, three times in the same chapter, warns us quite emphatically not to be deceived. It's important for us to take heed of this warning. We're pointing it out in this little book because the warning is so strong and comes from the Lord Himself.

If ever there was a time when we really need to read and understand the whole counsel of God—the entire Bible—these are the days now. The Word of God needs to be our textbook and teacher in these times and always.

If ever there was a time when we need to memorize Scripture, understand sound doctrine, and understand the importance of our statement of faith, it is now, as we head into the end-time scenario and the soon return of our Lord and Savior, Jesus Christ.

Is there anything we can do to protect ourselves against being deceived? Let me encourage you. Get to know the Word of God and the heart of God. Fall in love with Him and be filled with the Holy Spirit of truth. Embrace the Word and the Spirit together; they will carry you and me safely to Heaven's shores.

Since Jesus urges us to beware of deception, we need to understand how it presents itself in our culture. I've listed below some deceptive issues we as believers face today:

Hyper Grace

You hear people say things like, "Don't get religious," or, "Don't put me on a guilt trip," and they accompany these defensive statements with lots of excuses and justifications for bad and sinful behavior. These attitudes may be culturally current, but they are Christianity without a cross, and they are unbiblical.

There's No Hell

Some people deny the existence of a final judgment and hell, but the Bible makes it very clear that Heaven is real and hell is also real! (See the parable of the rich man and Lazarus in Luke 16:19-31, and many more references as well.)

False Prophecies

Don't be overly dependent on prophetic revelation without properly testing its source and without checking its credibility against the Word of God. First Thessalonians 5:20 says, *"Despise not prophesyings,"* and the next verse says, *"Prove all things; hold fast that which is good"* (KJV). All prophecy must be tested against the Word and checked for a witness (see 1 Cor. 14:29).

Sin Doesn't Matter

There is a belief that sin no longer matters. Why? Because "Jesus paid it all for you." Yes, He certainly did, but you cannot sin deliberately and hope God doesn't care or notice. When we sin knowingly, the Bible says we "trample the Blood of Christ underfoot" (see Heb. 10:29).

We can't say we love God if we walk in disobedience, because Scripture clearly says to love God is to obey Him (see John 14:21). Jesus is looking for a Bride without spot or wrinkle, without sin; a Bride who has made herself ready; a holy Bride for a holy King and a holy Kingdom of love.

The Bride is one who walks and behaves like Jesus did when He was on earth. She desires to walk in holiness. We need to talk more about holiness and the fear of the Lord, as well as His love, grace, and compassion.

The Greatest Deception

I think the greatest deception referenced here is for us to believe that the antichrist is actually the true Messiah who is to come.

The coming false prophet is committed to pushing this narrative to deceive multitudes of people and cause them to take the mark of the beast—the 666 of Revelation 13:18, whatever it turns out to be—and to actually worship him as god! People will be coerced into receiving his mark in order to buy and sell and carry on with life. We are witnessing a foreshadowing of this very conditioning today as those who refuse to be vaccinated are now losing their jobs and are unable to enter restaurants, sporting events, and even grocery stores. This false prophet will cause all to ultimately worship the antichrist, as foretold in Revelation 13:15: *"and cause that as many as would not worship the image of the beast* [antichrist] *should be killed"* (KJV).

I believe we are in the season of what the Bible calls the end times. Still, there is a needed balance to be sought and found, friend.

We know that Jesus is returning soon, but how soon? I have found that the Bible teaches us to hold these two conflicting possibilities in tension. Perhaps He could return today or this week. On the other hand, His return could be ten years away or even more. We need to plan our lives accordingly. Can you do that? Plan for two distinct possibilities?

Truly and sincerely expect Him *today*—Jesus could come for His Bride, the Church for whom He died, and set in motion every scenario that goes with His coming. For instance, the dead in Christ rising first:

Then we who are alive and remain [on earth] *shall be caught up* [raptured—*harpazo*] *together with them in the clouds to meet the Lord in the air. And thus we shall always be with the Lord* (1 Thessalonians 4:17).

What a thrilling climactic event that will be!

But meanwhile, until He comes, you and I need to carry on with our lives, living for Christ, sharing our faith, and finishing our education. We need to plan our career and marry and plan our family. Jesus admonished us to "do business" until He comes (see Luke 19:13). Perhaps it is difficult, but still very doable. Human nature would like to focus on one or the other, but no—we are told to do both together, letting His return be a sudden surprise.

So there it is, redeemed one! Are you going to be one who is deceived? Or are you going to remain true to the truths of orthodoxy? It is not really so difficult, not really: *"There is no other name under heaven given among men by which we must be saved"* (Acts 4:12).

Keep your eyes on Jesus, read and meditate on the whole counsel of God, hold fast your confession of faith! Fall in love (see Matt. 22:37), and get ready for the greatest event since the Creation!

ON EARTH PEACE

Glory to God in the highest,
and on earth peace, goodwill toward men!
(Luke 2:14)

Be encouraged, everybody!

The return of King Jesus to the earth to establish His Kingdom of righteousness is imminent. Truth and Love will finally be reestablished. It will be the greatest event since the Creation took place.

At the moment the whole earth is groaning and travailing for His coming again. The signs and evidences of His soon return are all around us.

The historical thumbnail sketch from Daniel 2 is behind us now—Israel is re-gathered as a nation since 1948, and Jerusalem is the undivided Jewish capital. The Gospel of the Kingdom has been preached to all the nations (see Matt. 24:14), yet I am troubled by this:

Why, then, are so many charismatic churches, pastors, and leaders not even mentioning the return of Christ? Friend, it is more sure than tomorrow's sunrise!

Where is the promise of His coming? Get ready, dear one! Live and plan your life to be sure, but also be ready:

So you also, when you see all these things, know that it is near—at the doors! (Matthew 24:33)

Now when these things begin to happen, look up and lift up your heads, because your redemption draws near (Luke 21:28).

Therefore be ye also ready: for in such an hour as ye think not the Son of man cometh (Matthew 24:44 KJV).

SCRIPTURES FOR MEDITATION AND CONTEMPLATION

Rapture Scriptures: Returning for His Bride, Delivering Us from Wrath

And to wait for His Son from heaven, whom He raised from the dead, even Jesus who delivers us from the wrath to come (1 Thessalonians 1:10).

For God did not appoint us to wrath, but to obtain salvation through our Lord Jesus Christ (1 Thessalonians 5:9).

So Christ was offered once to bear the sins of many. To those who eagerly wait for Him He will appear a second time, apart from sin, for salvation (Hebrews 9:28).

Because you have kept My command to persevere, I also will keep you from the hour of trial which shall come upon the whole world, to test those who dwell on the earth (Revelation 3:10).

But take heed to yourselves, lest your hearts be weighed down with carousing, drunkenness, and cares of this life, and that Day come on you unexpectedly. For it will come as a snare on all those who dwell on the face of the whole earth. Watch therefore, and pray always that you may be counted worthy to escape all these things that will come to pass, and to stand before the Son of Man (Luke 21:34-36).

And if I go and prepare a place for you, I will come again and receive you to Myself; that where I am, there you may be also (John 14:3).

His Ultimate Return: Second Coming and Christ's Kingdom on Earth

And in the days of these kings the God of heaven will set up a kingdom which shall never be destroyed; and the kingdom shall not be left to other people; it shall break in pieces and consume all these kingdoms, and it shall stand forever (Daniel 2:44).

Then to Him was given dominion and glory and a kingdom, that all peoples, nations, and languages should serve Him. His dominion is an everlasting dominion, which shall not pass away, and His kingdom the one which shall not be destroyed (Daniel 7:14).

And the Lord shall be King over all the earth. In that day it shall be—"The Lord is one," and His name one (Zechariah 14:9).

Then the righteous will shine forth as the sun in the kingdom of their Father. He who has ears to hear, let him hear! (Matthew 13:43)

Then the sign of the Son of Man will appear in heaven, and then all the tribes of the earth will mourn, and they will see the Son of Man coming on the clouds of heaven with power and great glory (Matthew 24:30).

Jesus said to him, "It is as you said. Nevertheless, I say to you, hereafter you will see the Son of Man sitting at the right hand of the Power, and coming on the clouds of heaven" (Matthew 26:64).

Then they will see the Son of Man coming in the clouds with great power and glory (Mark 13:26).

Jesus said, "I am. And you will see the Son of Man sitting at the right hand of the Power, and coming with the clouds of heaven" (Mark 14:62).

Then they will see the Son of Man coming in a cloud with power and great glory. Now when these things begin to happen, look up and lift up your heads, because your redemption draws near (Luke 21:27-28).

Who also said, "Men of Galilee, why do you stand gazing up into heaven? This same Jesus, who was taken up from you into heaven, will so come in like manner as you saw Him go into heaven" (Acts 1:11).

*And that He may send Jesus Christ, who was preached
to you before, whom heaven must receive until the times
of restoration of all things, which God has spoken by
the mouth of all His holy prophets since the world
began* (Acts 3:20-21).

*So that He may establish your hearts blameless in
holiness before our God and Father at the coming
of our Lord Jesus Christ with all His saints*
(1 Thessalonians 3:13).

*When He comes, in that Day, to be glorified in His
saints and to be admired among all those who believe,
because our testimony among you was believed*
(2 Thessalonians 1:10).

*Looking for and hastening the coming of the day of
God, because of which the heavens will be dissolved,
being on fire, and the elements will melt with fervent
heat? Nevertheless we, according to His promise, look for
new heavens and a new earth in which righteousness
dwells* (2 Peter 3:12-13).

Behold, He is coming with clouds, and every eye will see Him, even they who pierced Him. And all the tribes of the earth will mourn because of Him. Even so, Amen. "I am the Alpha and the Omega, the Beginning and the End," says the Lord, "who is and who was and who is to come, the Almighty" (Revelation 1:7-8).

He who testifies to these things says, "Surely I am coming quickly." Amen. Even so, come, Lord Jesus! (Revelation 22:20)

The grace of our Lord Jesus Christ be with you all. Amen.

APPENDIX B

OUR STATEMENT OF FAITH

We believe there is **one God** who lives forever in **three** persons: the Father, Son, and Holy Spirit (Matt. 28:19).

We believe that the **Bible is God's Word** to the world, speaking to us with authority and without error (2 Tim. 3:16-17).

We believe in the **divinity of Jesus Christ** the Son, His virgin birth, His sinless life, His miracles, His death for us on the cross, His bodily resurrection, His ascension to the Father, *and His personal, physical return to rule the earth in power and love* (John 1:14-18; 1 Thess. 4:16-18).

We believe that all **mankind is lost in sin** and needs to turn from it and trust personally in the Savior, Jesus Christ, through repentance and belief. All need to be born anew by the Holy Spirit's power into God's family (Eph. 2:1-10; John 3:5-7).

We believe the **Holy Spirit lives in us** as believers and brings love, joy, peace, patience, kindness, goodness, faithfulness, humility, and self-control into our lives. He gives us **spiritual gifts** including speaking in tongues, prophesying, and healing, among others (Gal. 5:22-23; 1 Cor. 12:7-11).

We believe in the resurrection of every person, to **eternal life** for the believer and eternal judgment for the lost (Matt. 25:31-46).

We believe in **unity for all believers** in our Lord Jesus Christ and seek community together—we want to become more like Him in every way, who is the head of His body, the Church. We are called to love Him and one another and are enabled to do this only as His life flows through us (1 Cor. 12:12-13; Matt. 22:37-40).

We believe the Scriptures teach that **marriage** is the covenanting together of **one man and one woman** in a union to the exclusion of all others (Gen. 2:18-25; Eph. 5:25-32).

ABOUT JOHN ARNOTT

John Arnott and his wife Carol are the Founding Pastors of the Catch The Fire Churches—the flagship church was formerly known as the Toronto Airport Christian Fellowship. As an international speaker, John has become known for his ministry of Revival in the context of the Father's saving and restoring Love. As the Holy Spirit moves with signs and wonders, he has seen millions of lives touched and changed through God's power and the love of Jesus.

Experience a personal revival!

Spirit-empowered content from today's top Christian authors delivered directly to your inbox.

Join today!
lovetoreadclub.com

Inspiring Articles
Powerful Video Teaching
Resources for Revival

Get all of this and so much more, e-mailed to you twice weekly!

LOVE TO READ CLUB
by **D** DESTINY IMAGE

Made in United States
Orlando, FL
04 December 2022

25512689R00063